Contents

BEING DRAGGED
ACROSS THE
CARPET
BY THE CAT

I CANNOT LIVE NOR DIE ANY LONGER
(Nem élhetek, se nem pusztulnak tovább)

For Miklós Radnóti

I build this
bridge of words

so that I can
walk back over time

and take
your hand.

You to me
this man

made only of
words

talking out of a book.

And I only able
to touch you

with these flawed words
of mine

I clasp your hand in mine
call you friend.

Miklós Radnóti, the Hungarian poet, was shot by guards after a forced march from a Serbian labour camp in 1944 and thrown into a mass grave. When his body was later exhumed, a notebook of poems was found sewn into his clothing so even from beyond this lonely grave his words insisted on living.

"Don't walk past me, friend. Yell, and I'll stand up again!"

I reach out my hand made of words and touch your words that still make you a man.

THE ME I AM

I laugh with a dead man's laugh
(a man I never knew)

my grandfather's laughter flowering like Springtime
blossoming in my mouth...not listening to the years.

Time joins the dots.
Painting by Numbers.

I see with my mother's eyes
the world stealing into my mind

become music
anything it chooses.

Time joins the dots.
Painting by numbers.

This gesture is my big sister's
gathering me up into her

nearness...tenderness.

Time joins the dots.
Painting by Numbers.

My father's love beats in my heart
sings in everything it touches

amuses me to see how I
am all those others as well as me.

Time joins the dots.
Painting by Numbers.

THE MAKING OF ME

Now, I am. . .
19,584 days old.

So, counting...
backwards

that means
on a Sunday in 1955

(23rd of Oct to be
precise)

me Ma & Da
(instead of taking their Sunday rest)

were busy
conceiving me.

So, that
on Sunday July 1956

I came about
(I came out)

& surrendered myself
to the world.

BIRTH STORIES

Before we knew
anything at all about sex

we knew all about our birth
stories.

Our Mam would recall & regale us all
(setting the table...peeling spuds...sweeping out the hall)

with the intimate details
of all our births.

"Tell us of US again...Mam...tell of us again! "

I was small (2lbs 2 ounces)
hardly anything at all.

A mere scrap of human being.

Bláthin Ashling was even smaller
(1 lb something or other)

...a little miracle.

Was it Deirdre with the cord wrapped
around her neck

fighting both Life & Death
'til she was blue in the face

Or Grainne with the cord so thin
she was born just in the nick of time

& the cord(just a hair's breath)

floats eternally now
(in a glass of formaldehyde still)

for doctors to astonish & marvel at.

And how. there being no incubators
when I came into being

they had to wrap me up in cotton wool

(as if I were a precious thing)
in order to keep me warm

but I wasn't having any of it
kicking my way out of the stuff

only for them to repackage
me again! And again...& again.

And here(in 1956)
I arrive on the scene

tiptoeing out into Life
with cool coal black full length sideburns

ready to rock & roll man
as the labour ward radio played

the hit of the day *"CE SERA...SERA! "*

It's almost as if I can still hear Doris singing
our *whatevers* will *bes.*

Our birth story each our first fairy story
& we

the Princes & Princesses of it. . .
all.

MY MOTHER'S HANDS

My mother's hands
washing potatoes washing kids washing pans.

My mother's hands on bitterly cold days
pegging yet more washing on a pregnant line

the line growing nothing but nappies
her hands blind with the cold.

My mother's hands
ironing clothes ironing clothes
ironing countless knickers for my seven sisters.

My mother's hands taking my hands in hers
such love...such laughter!

My mother's hands patting talcum powder
on another baby's bum.

Mum being Mum.

Me, kissing my mother's hands
for all...they've done.

BETWEEN THE SPACE

When I was small
I wanted - a pet.

My mother didn't
- like pets.

'It followed me home! '
'Can I...keep it...can I...can..! '

didn't work & I invariably had to
return the kidnapped cat

to the house I had
'borrowed' him from.

Between the space

where my mother wrung
screamingwetclothesthroughtherollers

and out the other side to quiet flatness

and the coal bunker

where a briquette wire spat at me
almost nearly blinding my left eye

I captured a Cabbage White
hiding amongst the coal.

Emptying the strawberry jam with the gollywog on

I gave her a world of glass where she danced
to the sunlight's mad music.

Neither she nor I
understanding the nature of glass

her dancing grew frantic
my love stifling.

I not knowing all things must breathe
. . .the dancing died to a sudden stop.

Being an impressionable child
and after only seeing a life safety film

I dived through the panic
and swam madly against the guilt

took her gently into my trembling fingers
...her dusty colour taking my fingerprints

I tried to give her the kiss of life

choked with grief
and swallowed her

terror in my mind butterfly in my tummy
and fear running blind and crazy

that I could not give her
her dancing back again.

I said nothing for years (about the incident)

until I could explain myself to myself
and my self ... understood.

NEVER SO ALONE AS HERE

A night
scattered with stars

each star so clear
in its perfect isolation

you feel as if you could pluck it from its position
examine it...put it exactly back

watch as time & the world come apart
(watch as neither match)

each minute like a bead of prayer
fumbled through fingers

in its litany of despair
a rosary of hopelessness

the back of her hand
resting in the palm of mine

stupidly the thought crossing my mind
"She made this hand..."

And now she searches for her dying
sees it reflected in our faces

our grief her mirror

each star a tear
in the perfection of its isolation

never so alone as here...as now

the Milky Way
spilt across the sky.

ME MAM'S MIND

"If you fall off that wall & break both your legs
...don't come running to me! "

Could never understand
my Mam's mind & how it worked.

One moment she "had half a mind
to come up there "& '"get me off that wall."

Then she "was in two minds
about' whether to tell me to stop.

"Go ahead...go ahead & kill yourself ...see if I care!"

"I'm warning you child if you fall off that wall & kill yourself
I'll personally come up there & murder ya myself so I will! "

I used to watch the words climbing out of her mouth
& fly around the room looking for a place to land

in my mind.

Never cared whether she gave out.
I just loved everything she said

the music of her & how
she made the words behave.

I came down and kissed her
kissed her worry away.

'I'm sorry Mam'
I told her.

And she cried.

- NO DIRECTIONS

South of Sorrow
North North West of Pain

I search for you &...
...lose you yet again.

I calculate your absence
by the stars

& you are near
though you are far.

I wander through this Wilderness of Loss
...is this what loving you has cost?

East of Loneliness
West of Grief

... If only for one brief

... your voice echoes inside my head

... I see you smile & laugh

... pretend that you're not dead.

...pretend that you're not dead.

CRAZY CANARY YELLOW

Bright skin - tight
a crazy canary yellow

jeans
my pride & joy

(my first Versace)

took a lot of balls
to wear 'em but then

I got 'em!

My mother hated
(with a vengeance)

them
(hated to pieces)
them

until one morning early
up with the crow of the cock

I cut them
myself to pieces

"Snick snack! " sniggered the scissors
(good for a laugh)

threw the shreds of the threads
up upon the roof

let an hour or so pass

and then discovering
my own (the devil's) handiwork

accused her
of the dastardly deed.

Who else(I said)....wanted the jeans dead?

Who hated *them* with such a passion
to do such...such a thing.

Maybe she thought...
“I did it in my (God forgive) sleep.”

“Although I know I didn’t do it
it’s what I would have wanted done.”

After hours struggling like a worm
I let her off the hook

confess it was I that done *them*
(the jeans) in.

She annoyed at the spoof that took her in
but delighted at the demise of

". . .those damn things."

The hearty laugh of then
the feeble smile of now

as she (here in this hospital)
tries not to die.

JESUS CHRIST IS ALIVE AND WELL

She is thoroughly wet
through & through

as if a someone(I don't know who)
had upended over her a bucket of water.

(The rain holds
a conversation with itself.)

"Where's your new coat? "
we incredulously ask her

as she continues to drip at us.

(The rain is laughing
at something it has told itself.)

"A poor woman hadn't one...
...so I gave her mine."

She explains as to a child
whilst we her children stare at her

hair plastered to her skull
a large drip at the end of her nose.

My mother could be kind
in an almost Biblical New Testament way

as if she were Jesus Christ
before he had gotten himself crucified

and was alive and well and living in her.

MEETING MY MOTHER

Here, I meet
my mother

before she has even thought of me.

Here, she a turning
twenty something or other

& I only the long longed for. . .

the sly shy twinkle
in her eye.

And now I am
her little boy

playing with photographs
scattered across sunshine linoleum.

Here now, I
a twenty something or other

& here I am older than she
was then

meeting my mother
in the spilt photographs

that scatter time
across this Autumn floor.

MA & PA & US

Her voice ran out to meet us
before she did

her singing gathering us up
held invisibly in each note

as if already we were a bunch
of flowers in her hand

before she pulled us close to her cuddly warmness
all breasts & softness

my mother's love enclosing us
as if she were prepared to die for us.

She the mother hen and we her precious chicks,
cliché though it is.

My Dad's bicycle bell & laughter
conjuring him up before he turned the corner

and presented himself to us
as if he were the most wonderful present

we could ever desire.

His love
all full of fun and songs and yet more laughter.

Us kids stood enraptured captivated by these beings

and their out-of-this-world...

love.

CHANGE OF ADDRESS

You didn't die
you just changed shape

became invisible
to the naked eye

became this grief

it's sharpness
more real

than your presence was

before you were separate to me
entire to yourself

now you are
a part of me

you are inside my self

I call you
by your new name

'Grief...Grief! '

although I still call you
'Love.'

DURING WIND & RAIN

Old bedraggled typewriter

emerging from the tangle of Time & weeds
its rotted ribbon still a defiant banner

held aloft in the war of the years
black bleeding into red

this maker of words creator of worlds
an angry E key rusted into a raised fist ready to strike

(a corroded gesture) stilled in time
its question mark missing

my fingerprints still adhering to some faded letters
still remembering my mind though grounded now

in earth & dog shit...a fallen leaf taking the page's place.

Here at the center of my garden I leave you to your fate
rusted into sculpture or symbol

where the seasons like ghosts visit you
speaking only in memories

here you now throwing off your cloak of snow
to encounter yet another summer

writing now the wind & rain that passes through you
singing your dearest songs(though hardly any hear you)

writing now of Time with nothing but time
offering me these words

like a prayer to the dying as I bring you back to life
this one last. . .time.

BACK IN THE HIGH LIFE AGAIN

I carry you before me
carefully cradled in interlaced fingers

like a pregnant mum would.

My shadow mimics the illusion.
My silhouette making me look

like I'm 7 months gone.

Pregnant with you
I carry you our Mum

transformed into this box
your life now nothing but these ashes

a number (2731)
our memories trying to keep you alive.

I place you on my lap...buckle up
(car pulling away from crematorium)

as your car-driving-song comes on
Steve Windwood's voice emerges from the speakers

like an arc of a diver
and you're *BACK IN THE HIGH LIFE AGAIN*

cradled between our
tears & laughter.

BEING DRAGGED ACROSS THE CARPET BY THE CAT

You fall on the floor.

Carefully I brush you up.

Returned to your urn

you sit upon the mantelpiece

gazing at the setting sun.

ADAGIO

the music
tiptoes

through
the room

careful not to
wake the sleeping

photographs
of the dead

their lives
trapped behind glass

amongst vast fields
of wallpaper violets

stopping to
caress

the singular
beauty

of the rose
dreaming

in its chipped
vase

of the garden
where it was born

curtains led
by a breeze

into their dance

gazing upon the green

that unfurls
about the house

the music
wounded now

by a tear
that grown upon

her cheek
note by note

a woman staring into space

the cat asleep
upon her toes

the music retreating
back into the mahogany cabinet

curling itself
into its circle

a whirlpool of black
shellac

the music
lost in the silence

only its breathing audible now
in the runoff groove

the needle returning
to its proper place

with a click
the last light
stealing across the lawn.

I AM AMAZON

topless bather
one tanned proud breast
the other - white scar

unashamed of her
solitary breast
'I AM AMAZON!" she proclaims

the next year
the other breast is lost
she bares her chest to all

topless
breast-less
she smiles at being alive

"I offer myself to the sun
sans emblems of woman
I spit in the cancer's face!"

dressed in only
birdsong
caressed by sun.

THE FINAL WORD

after the accident
her rather forward sloping writing
now leans back

the once firm hand
now a spiderly crawl
across the blue page

"When you read this I will be
dead. . "
letter from beyond the grave

the Past & the Present
collapse
into each other

the voice
so alive
the letter shakes

"...even though I'm gone
I just
wanted to have the final word. . ."

written in blue *Quink* ink
teardrops dissolve
her words

her chair
as if she had just
(left there)

it seeming
as if she had just
(stepped out of the room)

everywhere
she wasn't
there she was.

I keep just missing her
blinded by tears I
stumble from room to room.

I call her name
a bird answers
rain taps on the pane

cupped in my palms
your memory
precious as water

I carry you
trying not to spill
a single drop

you slip
through my fingers
like time...time

I press my palms
to my eyes
nothing but tears

Spring happens without you
I stare with disbelief
at your death

LISTENING TO YOUR FAVOURITE PIECE OF MUSIC

Oh you were so quiet

I hardly heard you tiptoe silently in
settle yourself amongst the strings

talking to me
now in cello now in violin
the heartbeat of a drum

the exchange of laughter
between glockenspiel & xylophone

making a point with either
the tiny tinkle of a triangle

or the crash of a cymbal.

I listen to you talk to me in music
the candlelight grows dim & then

as softly as you came. . .you leave

leaves

(fluttering against
the windowpane)

I feel you leave
leave before the movement ends

footsteps
in the silence of my memory

me nearly forgetting that you've died
listening on until the end as the music

cries....

YOU CAN CALL ME... AL

As your cancer twists & snarls
biting into your soul

it gnaws away at my name
the pain unable to pronounce it

DÓNALL

becomes

...ÓNALL.

Then. . .*NALL.*

Until your dying day
I become simply

. . .*AL.*

SLOVO LJUBAVI
(THE WORD OF LOVE)

Here I am
nailed to this hated bed

with the bright shiny
nails of cancer.

Death smiles
& wants to take me

as his bride
but I remain unfaithful to him

elope with life
(if only for this night)

spending golden moments
as if there were no

tomorrow.

I fling my laughter
in his big stupid grinning face

as if he thinks this is all a human is
a something to be taken.

I hope to sneak out when he is not looking
or looking the other way

before he discovers me alive in your heart
(untouchable)

my memory
safe in your memory

so that to kill me
he will have to kill you too.

So beware my friend

you will become
a marked man

& Death cheated of my soul
will hunt you down

and rip me from your heart
to finish the job.

But I know you will
hide me

hide me among your words
little seeds of me

that will propagate
so that Death would have to kill the whole world.

I laugh to see
the little seedlings of me

sprout in other minds
other voices

see my laughter blossom
on a strange tongue

unknown to me but known,

Death furiously glaring.

FAIRY TALE

I sit by your bedside
watching your dying.

Only Love
nails me to this pain,

I unable to escape your dying.

I tell you Irish legends
& Hans Christian Anderson

as you become again
(if only for a little while)

the child you used to be
once upon a time

when wonder & delight
were new as daylight.

"Tell me Lir! "
"Tell me the Children of Lir! "

I tell of how

they are turned into swans
& the loneliness of eternity.

I too knit nettles to break the spell
throw the garment over your cancer'd body

so you can return again
to being

the human I have known.

This dying is cruel beyond belief,
an insult to your life.

I love you so much I would kill you
if I could kill you but I...can't.

I want every breath of you
not to be your last.

You journey to your death
dancing with your pain

my little mermaid
my little ballerina

I guard your dying
a Constant Tin Soldier

as you become foam
foam on the sea.

Just a day ago
sucking a sultana

I held on the tip of my fingertip
telling me to call your name.

"I love living in your voice! "
"So nice...so nice! "

And I a blind Prince

wandering now lost
in the fairy tale of your Death.

I close your eyes.
Kiss the last warmth of your lips.

YOUR SHOES

Your shoes
all stand together

lined up like a chorus line
in the bottom of your wardrobe.

These your "dancing" ,
these your "kiss me kiss me shoes"

these your plod around the house
"doin' nuthin' shoes"

these your "carefree
who gives a....shoes. "

The shoes
chatter amongst themselves

remembering all the different YOUs
you could be.

Your dresses float above them
like dreams your shoes dreamed.

Tomorrow
they will learn of your death,

packed away
in black refuse sacks,

beginning their new life
in a charity shop.

THAT PLACE CALLED DAY

Later when I looked for you
(you were gone)

you had turned into Time

your hair turned into time
your tears turned into Time

nothing I could hold
nothing I could touch

(Love trying to hold
on to everything)

as the winds of Time
...blew it all away.

I walked away into that place
called Day

(you know that place)
between morning & night

that place where you
no longer are

that place that you have left
that place where you exist

only
in my mind.

SWEET

The day she went
out of our lives

I offered her a sweet.

'Thanks love, I'll eat it
later on the bus.'

She snaps it shut in her little red purse.

I still feel my hand letting go of her hand
see for the last time her never-again-seen face.

Only the little red purse returns
out of its mouth...Death laughs

in blood besprinkled glass
some small change...the never eaten sweet.

For years it lives behind the wind-up clock
in my mother's bedroom

scaring me each time I have to pass
and it sees me   and laughs.

My little brother not even born then when...
jumps up & down playing alone

all by himself
in a world of his own.

He is both good guy & bad guy
falling down dead on the bed

as a quick spat out shot
ricochets & agggh...gits him!

Even by 7
killing yourself is a tiring business.

He stops. Rests.

...rummages around among
my mother's artifacts.

His little inquiring mind
snaps open the little red purse.

Death laughs(but he not knowing)
is immune to it.

He sees the white wrapped death sweet
almost glowing against the red.

He sees it...eats it.

The Past has been
eaten by the Present.

Unaware of what he has done
(Death defeated)

he flings himself on the bed once again
pretending he is dead

sunlight streams through the glass
holds him gently in its hand

this the living child
Death dead at last.

GLASS

Only her red purse returns.

Inside it a sweet

some small change &
blood besprinkled glass.

It alone survives the crash.

Death is only a newspaper headline.

Still...this grief!

I weep tears that don't show up
on my face.

I push my fingers
deep in the purse

trying to get near you
cut my fingertips to bits

the held glass
(all I have of you)
scarring my face

blind to the pain.

The old blood and the new mingles
and once more

if only for a second
we are together
for as long as the pain lasts.

YOUR LAUGHTER LOST AMONG BALLOONS

Your hand pins the Santa
to the living room door

his belly blossoming into decoration
your eyes alive with Christmas lights

blinking on & off

your laughter lost
among balloons

floating in an other world
& yet another Christmas

the same scene re-enacts itself
(without your presence)

presents lolling mutely
around the festive tree

each detail crystal clear
the dance of your hands...the music of your hair

turning ever turning

sharp as holly
drops of blood mimicking its berries

I suck my thumb to staunch the flow

memories red & real
as blood

Death sitting in your empty chair.

BIG SISTER

You were older than me
now I am older than you

can ever be

(forever 18 & forever dead) .

I felt so guilty when I passed that age
wishing I could exchange some of the life I had

so that you could experience
the life you never knew.

I used to talk to your grave as if it were you...
Always beginning: "Hiya, kid..."

Now I find you everywhere instead
the sunlight on the garden smiles like you did

the ladybird stumbling
over the furrows of my fingerprint

has the same graceful awkwardness
your body lent to every movement.

You are younger than me & will always be.

And I am older than you
...will ever know..

SNOWSTORMS

It was the most magical thing
I'd ever seen....a winter scene

with a stumpy little snowman leaning on a broom
and snow-coloured trees.

The snowman was always smiling.

Then the world shock and turned upside down
and the blizzard began again.

Snowflakes falling in slow motion.
I wanted them to fall forever.

My sister smiling at my: "Again...again! "
turned the little glass world upside down

and once again the snowflakes fell
so slowly suspended in time.

I smiled at the snowman smiling.
My sister smiled at me.

I would spend time after time
forever after

playing with suspended Time
stopping the world to begin it again.

One day it fell(shattered)
and spilled out all

across the lace table cloth
lapping at the evil smelling geraniums.

The snowman was plastic
(and the snow was plastic too) .

Time poured itself out to the edge of the table
& drip by drop

pooled itself on the living room floor.

Time was only an illusion
its mystery nothing more than

my tears crying for what could never be again.

Somewhere in Time

a bus is crashing.

I can still see my sister smiling...

...a world falling out of her hand.

CRASH

Her body lay broken
shattered by the crash

like a mirror scattered
reflecting only that she had left

left her pulse beating madly
into the darkness

left her breath faltering
into the shadows

left her heart beating
without a moment

to hold her self in...to see her self in

her eyes letting go of the sky becoming sunset

her hands letting go of the memories
that would forget her

her mouth seeking kisses of those
who had loved her

& she abandoned this life
because. . .Death had asked her.

SWEET (LITTLE RED PURSE)

See the purse. Little red purse. Little red purse with golden clasp. Snap it shut. See June open the purse. Open the purse June. Snaps shut. Sweet. How sweet? Surrounded by toffee the soft chocolate waits to be bitten into.

'Not now love, I'll have it later.'

The bus is late. We all wait. In school we chanted 'Here comes the bus...here comes the bus...will there be room for all of us? ' We all wait. The bus is late. She laughs with her friend. See June laugh. Laugh June laugh. Her hair eclipses her eyes. Her eyes vanish in her laughter. She had given me money to buy sweets as we wait for the late bus. She is totally absorbed in the words her friend is mouthing.

I can only see her talk. I can't seem to hear her anymore. Memory erases itself. The only sound is silence. I am offering her a sweet. She takes it absentmindedly and smiles: 'Not now love, I'll have it later.' She clicks open her little red purse. The white sweet curls up and sleeps.

The bus puffs and pants. It creeps and crawls up the hill. Junie's laughter freezes into slow motion. Laughter spills like water. Splashes me. I am totally absorbed in her being totally absorbed with the laughter. The world is only 'now.' Now is all there is. The bus takes a millennium to arrive at where we are. It has to crawl from the world of time into our world of no time. Yet in no time at all the bus is no longer there. It is a dot in the distance - a curtain of trees eclipsing it as it turns a bend. Gone.

I am letting go of her hand. My hand is waving goodbye. Her hand is waving goodbye. There is only the dance of hands. The language of gesture. Her face floats and bobs away from me forever. I never see her again. Memory starts to erode reality. I only remember that I forget.

The water splashes all over me. I am washing myself in the sink. The knock on the door freezes the water... the moment... and who I am. When the strange man leaves my world...my world no longer exists. The bus crashes. See the bus crash. Crash bus crash. Look Dónall look!

'Here comes the bus...here comes the bus! '

Bric-a-brac floats back. The little red purse returns. It is snapped shut. Its innocence survives death. Its casual simplicity is intact. All facts are kept from the purse. All is contained in its redness. For years it lays unnoticed...unopened. It lives in the space behind the clock that tolls the time. The hours resonate as they pass. The purse has transformed itself into clutter. It is only another item that fills up space. It has no function other that to have no function. It is opened casually and by sheer chance.

Death spills out. Splashes me all over. Little bits of glass flecked with blood glint in the new light of an other 'now.' A different 'now.' I cut myself shutting it. Fresh blood. The white sweet still lies asleep curled up into it self. Its whiteness shocking against the sheer redness.

Death is a seven year old uneaten sweet. Death glints ready to cut again. For years it inhabits yet another existence...the existence of never opening again. It has a power all of its own. I cut across a room rather than confront it. Frantically looking for something or other I suddenly confront it. It confounds me and wounds me with its presence.

My little brother enacts a film he has recently seen. He plays all the parts. Suddenly, he the good guy, is shot by the bad guy who is also himself. He clutches his heart in disbelief...stammers in a bad Bogie voice: 'Ya got me...kid! ' He grabs the purse in order to signify his deathly wound. He holds it to his heart where it apparently bleeds through his fingertips. This purse means Death. I leave him dying over my mother's bed.

Although he is now dead his curiosity gets the better of him. He is hungry and teatime is a far away place. The purse opens with a slight gasp from its golden clasp. The white sweet reveals itself - a deadly pearl held in red. Somewhere in time a bus is crashing. Hands are waving goodbye. June is laughing. She clicks her purse shut. The bus has not appeared as yet- the bus has just come into view. There is only now...this moment. Timeless.

'Not now love...'

My little brother sees it.

It is a Cadbury's Chocolate Éclair.

There is only one sweet.

There is only one of him.

There is only one thing to do.

He eats it.

BIG SISTER IS TELLING LITTLE BROTHER A POEM

Kisses
like Japanese paper flowers

opening upon
touching water

blossoming into amazement
to bloom for ever in imagination

your breath

(lace curtains dancing in the breeze)

carries carefully each word
letting it break fragile as a bubble

gently against my skin
your voice settling and unsettling my hair

the poem rising and falling
borne upon your breathing

like petals upon a stream

cuddled into you
a dream of a dream

forever you telling poem upon poem

your heart beating preciously
against my heart

I understanding completely
your mind...is my home.

THE SOUND OF HER

The sound of my sister's voice.

We lived in a house not made of books. The only texts existed in the texture of the telling...my sister finecombing my hair and soothing the pain with ...shussh...stories.

'The little toy soldier is covered with dust...'

...exists only in my mind and the vague trellised traces of Junie's voice. It is here breath against my skin as I fall asleep. It has never entered my mind through print yet it is printed irredeemably...indelibly in my mind.

'What is it again? '

I am following my father...dogging my Dad doggedly for the words of a song. I scrawl the words across the page of my mind as exasperated his patience explodes:

'As down the bloody glen one bloody Easter morn...how many times do I have to tell you! '

My sister Moira is slightly tipsy. I glow with pleasure as the pattern unfolds. When she is more than slightly tipsy she will softly and sadly sing.

'I know my love by his way of walking and I know my love by his way of talking and I know my love by his eyes so blue and if my love left me what would I do...? '

I am drunk with her words. There is a slight smell of loneliness off her breath. I hang on her every breath.

I have had four teeth pulled and my world fevers and frets. The smell of sausages sidles up the stairs and seduces me to the top of the stairs. When I am safely in danger the smelly magic no longer supports me. I fall and float down the stairs.

Junie comforts and croons. I am lying in her arms in her bed. Again she sings. 'Again! ' I plead. She sings again.

'Black is the colour of my true love's hair...her lips are like...'

Her body vibrates with sound and the words echo through me and echo through the memory of me.

For a long long time the only way these words were written down was in the breath entering and leaving her body.

When I remember to write...

I write to remember I write to forget.

I write to recover what has never left me but exists in a someplace of my mind. I write to find out who I am and if I ever was.

I write to discover where I went when the world went away.

As the bus crashes the book is torn and burning. The world dies. A child cries.

The book lies strewn across the motorway. Its spine is broken and its leaves flutter away in dismay. The book is burning. It is unreadable as it reads itself to the night's wind. It is an image torn from a dream that is really real. Its spine is broken and pages turn themselves over and over in the night.

I write...to remember...I write...to forget.

Sunlight streams through the bedroom window...sculpts a sister. Creates Junie. She is telling me the story of Orpheus and Eurydice.

Every time I cry. She says she will not tell me again because it always me makes me cry. I promise not to cry if she promises to tell me again. She tells me again. I cry every time. She is not

dead. She is telling me the story of Orpheus and Eurydice. She is created of sunlight. Dust motes dance in attendance. It cannot be...more real than this.

I write to remember...I write...to forget. I write to recover the times of her not dying...when she is sunlight and breath. When she was my book.

When the sound of her was all...around me.

Writing to remember...I forget so much. I write because I am - lost. I write to find an exit door in my mind. The book is broken. The book is burning. Pages...fiery pages flutter like lost souls escaping into the darkness.

I write to reach the light. I write to enter the darkness. I write to escape the sound of the book burning.

I write to forget...I...write to...not forget.
Remember. . .

TIME WAS

The poem
only exists on your breath

in the rise and fall of your telling.

It will be another 40 years
before I see it written in a book

...and tears come unbidden.

I a little boy
crying for a little boy blue

who tells his toys to wait for him
until the morning comes...

but being good Victorian melodrama
the little boy dies.

Still the toys wait...

for the touch of his hand

...that will never come.

In the real live boy
that I am

there isn't a dry eye
and I cry and cry the house down.

You kiss & cuddle me.

Your death
traps me in this poem

and melodrama becomes real

& I cry now
as a man

...this poem only exists
on the nearness of your breath

& I forever tell it
to your ghost.

****

***** Eugene Field's poem "LITTLE BOY BLUE" is interwoven into my life and I actually came to live it for real...it is made not only with words but death and grief and the memory of my lost sister's voice. It doesn't exist as a text or a page for me but only in that telling all those years ago and the ghost of that memory.**

MEETING W.B. YEATS FOR THE FIRST TIME

Curled up in a cuddle

fused into
the one telling the one listening

my big sister
recites Yeats

She whispers:

"Come away o human child..."

as the thunderstorm breaks outside
"...to the waters and the wild..."

as the night breaks open
over the poem

"...to a world more full of weeping..."

the lightning illuminates each line
"...than you will ever understand..."

I cry into her body great heaving sobs
And she says: "Shhh...shhh.. it's alright! "

and I only half believe her
her death etched into my mind.

SKIN & BLISTER

We grin & grimace
drop candle wax onto our fingertips

as the storm
rattles our window pane

angry that we won't let it in.

All night it rages
toppling chimney pots with a crash

smashing slates
it strips from rooftops

as we safe
giggle & peel off

our waxen
fingerprints

hold them
(tiny whirlpools)
in our palms

those whorls of self
unique to each.

I wearing my sister's
fingerprints

she... wearing mine.

STOLEN LAUGHTER

My soul disguised as a shadow
drifted back into my past

managed unseen to cross
the border of Life (& Death)

enter again that room where the memory begins
(when the memory wasn't even a memory)

but the real thing

my soul steals a crumb of her laughter
nothing that could be missed

the merest sliver. I (then) shiver
seeing my soul stealing my sister's laughter

but not recognising it
seeing only a shadow of a shadow.

Throwing off its shadowy clothes
my soul returns smelling remotely of a Past
the stale smell of Death.

"Did you get it...did you get it! "
I demand.

"Yes...yes...but don't ask me again! "
"If God ever finds out..."

But I don't hear
I am beyond my soul's reproach

following the steps of my tears
leading me to

the treasure of her
laughter.

KISSING THE DOT

Our new black & white
more full of snow than pictures

holding the rabbit's ears just so
("No...no...no...YES! ! ! ! ! ! !")

holding it aloft like a 9 year old Statue of Liberty
watching with fascination as *I DREAM OF JEANIE*

emerges
to our chorused 'ooooOOOOO! '

Even turning it off was a thrill
the little white dot dwindling to an infinity

the electric static tingling our lips
as we kissed it goodbye

. . .a pleasurable pain.

Now, after the bus crash
lost in staticky snow

I turn the set
on off onoff

watch the little white dot
die again and again

place my lips
against the fading screen

the electric kiss
of death.

KYO NO TOBIRA

(TODAY'S DOOR)

A SEQUENCE

MUMONKAN (GATELESS PASS)

Here, now
sister mine

lost
in time

dead to this world

I offer you

my eyes
my ears

so that you can see...can hear
without fear of Death

always interrupting you.

Take this breath & live again.
I can see enough for two.

MYOJU (THE END OF LIFE)

After the bus crash her soul walked home
limping awkwardly now

leaving a trail of footprints
leaking time like blood.

KAEI (THE SHADOWS OF FLOWERS)

Often, I visit this moment
long gone

(that has never ceased to exist) .

I go to find my sister
calling her name

lost as she is in the middle
of this vast field

her blue dress a flower

at the very center of it.

Here, Death
does not know her

name
only I call her.

She carries me home
in a piggyback.

I fascinated with the freckle
under the shadow of a curl

where shoulder
meets neck.

I lost in her laughter.

Both of us escaping
her Death.

AME NO UTA (SONGS OF RAIN)

Here, Death
itemises her.

The bruised breast.
The torn spleen.
The broken ribs.
The haemorraging.

Death, leaving
his mark

on this
human being.

Familiar with her.
Owning her.

Memory tiptoes
into Death's great palace

& steals back
a freckle

lost behind
a curl

between
shoulder
& neck.

Death
has no need

for it.

THE SOUL GOES FOR A STROLL

My Uncle sleeps with pursed lips
as if kissed by a dream.

Perched upon this kiss
a butterfly sits

as if an Uncle's lips were the most natural
place for a butterfly to rest

or as if it were an illustration
of the soul

a symbol in a magical book
that explained such things.

Outside the trees breathe gently
inhaling & exhaling a soft whisper of wind.

Bees carve a map out of the air
for other bees to see.

Out on a limb
two birds sit & chit chat.

A fox(unseen)passes by
as if it had never been.

A big big bug topples off the top
of a tiny stone onto its back

wriggling its arms & legs
as if it were trying to swim

through the currents of its fear.

One of the gossiping birds

sees him as a tasty treat.

Eats him.

Inside the house's
El Greco shadows

a kitten exploring the newness
of the world it finds itself in

jumps onto the sleeping statue
of an Uncle

with a butterfly
perched upon its lips.

Kitten tumbles ooops
into my Uncle's crotch

before climbing the mountain side
that is his chest.

Takes a swipe at the soul
pretending to be a butterfly

just as my Uncle
awakens to this reality

& his soul flits just
out of reach

between the fireplace
& the mantelpiece.

DIRECTIONS

I'm heading West
(where ever that is) .

I march off into the distance
of field & sky.

West is where
my uncle is.

I cut through
the heat haze.

My uncle's dinner
wrapped up in a scarf on the end of a stick

as if I am
running away into forever.

Tea slops in an old milk bottle
with a piece of cloth as a stopper.

I stare into the empty air
as if suddenly I will discover there

a sign saying:
"West – this way! "

My Auntie Nellie's instructions
still stamped on the inside of my stupid skull.

"Go west into the field
with your Uncle Michael's dinner.

"Tell him. . ."

Me too terrified to tell her
I don't know where West is?

Typical townie!

I search the farm field by field
'till I finally find him

sprouting out of a field
with a cloud attached to his head

beside the broken rickety gate
where the tiniest ever wild strawberries grow.

So this is where West is!

Why didn't she say so in the first place!
This I know!

Why send me like a fool on a child's errand!

My uncle devours everything 'cept
the scarf & the stick.

Tells me
("Oh no! ")

to go South to where Uncle Seanie is

and. . .

UNCLE MICHAEL - ALIAS GOD

His hands (tobacco stained)
twisted & gnarled

knotted like an alive piece of wood
scrawled gestures across my mind

as the sick calf bucked in his arms
& his quiet strength - calmed:

'Shhhhhh... shhhhhhh...suck...suck! '
he crooned

& the sound soothed.

And the veins (line vines)
ran up & down his arms

pumping crude life like a sudden sketch
to suggest the gist of rather than

the meaning of things.

And he walked (& I ran)
towards Granny's garden (like God tending Eden)

& the gate (a little hoarse) sighed at his hand and

the leaves murmured
(like worshippers in a church congregation)

& the sunlight genuflected through the trees
and the trees wore socks & apples.

A tablecloth was laid on a loganberry bush.

And the young tree gave herself to him
broke tenderly in his hand

and the knife whistled & whittled
& out of the branch came a man.

And he told me (& I believed him
'cos he was good as God & strong)

that the little wooden man (the silent statue)
had been waiting (all the time all ready made)

waiting to be released
from his prison of wood.

'All things...'he whispered
'all things are waiting for you to call them.'

'Call them to come out...'
'Awake them...create them...! '

The rhododendrons were blue with amazement

at this revelation
a dragonfly walked upon the water.

A butterfly became infatuated with a flower.

Me...?

I watched as his hands talked
explaining things that could not be...said.

And he took my hand in his and I understood

flowed like a little stream into his big river

felt God (close)
near at hand

and...smiling.

CENTAUR

Hiding in the hay
me a terrified little boy
& my uncle like a terrified little boy

the voices in his head telling him to be afraid
of all strangers...changes.

He's been like this
since the day his Dad(my unknown grandfather)
died.

My Aunt's voice
searching for us...searching us out.

Her shouts like bloodhounds
hunting us down

her words sneery & cruel.

Her angry voice slurring us into:
"DonallSeanie! "

as if we had fused into one being
a metamorphosis of us.

The hay cooks us
and we swelter in our hidey-hole.

A chicken sits on top
of my uncle's cap

as if his mind had
materialised into this shape.

He rocks himself
and rocks me.

"Shhhh...boy...shhhh! "

comforting both him & me.

"Don't leave me! "
he clucks

the words scattered around him
like newly laid eggs.

I settle into his silence.

My Aunt's threats freezing us
in this terrible heat.

His chest hair
tickles my nose.

The cut on my left big toe
throbs through the open sandal.

My uncle cries in fear.

I wipe away the tear
with the dirty edge of my sleeve.

We escape to the West field
me riding his shoulders

transformed into
a legendary creature

that only exists in myths
fleeing from the realness

...of reality.

GOODBYE TO THE CIRCUS

'Oh! Nellie the elephant packed her trunks and said goodbye
to the circus...off she went with a clumpity clump... clump
....clump... clump! The head of the herd was calling...
far far away.'

Auntie Nellie
died of:

drink, loneliness: & whatever...

(not necessarily in that order) .

And the farm that was
our young days summer holidays

cast her youth like so much pig slop
to the squelching grunt of

cow dung days
moo cow lowing years

until the dust collected and
settled in the corners

no one could reach....

Time left her like a Holy Picture
high above the mantelpiece.

See the children take the coloured cards
in their hands

go play 'Fish in the Pool! '
Scream: 'Snap! '

Laugh at who is left to be:
'Old Maid! '

'Not me! '

'Not me! '

Time never took her
hand like a lover's touch.

Time only
waited for her.

In her loneliness
she read and re-read and lived on:

Aldous Huxley's - *ISLAND.*

She said...this said: 'Everything! '

Years, later...when she reads
like a fictional character

in someone's story

when time no more ...mattered.

I travelled to her
ISLAND

and touched her LONELINESS.
felt her LONGING.

Auntie Nellie died of:
drink, loneliness: and whatever

(not necessarily in that order) .

...said goodbye to the circus......calling far far away...

SAD VALENTINES FOR BREAKFAST

Oh my how red cock struts (thinks he's a sultan)
striding in and out among his harem-scarum hens

talking to themselves
like some lost senile sentimental souls.

Foolish fowl!

They lay eggs for gentlemen
and kids on long hot summer holidays

they hide their eggs like broken hearts
like old love letter secrets

safe in unseen places.

But see Auntie Nellie willy-nilly as a fox
stalk the chickens and expose them

cruel as the *NEWS OF THE WORLD.*

See her raid the haystacks
(back seat of the old car)
rain rusting machinery

her apron pregnant and precious with
the warm and brown gift of eggs.

Red cock crows loud against the morning marigolds
while children's voices babble sleepily into wide wakefulness

love letter secrets staining their lips
sad valentines for breakfast.

Granny's garden
she's in there somewhere
only her song visible

camouflaged by
her ripening gooseberries
Granny sings to the summer

I follow
the path of her
song

pillowcases & tea towels
drying on bushes & branches
Granny and the birds sing

I step on each note
a pathway
through the air

Granny's garden overgrown
with Time
her song still rests upon the air

Granny's garden
she's in there somewhere
hidden by Death

I step upon each note
still following
the pathway of her song

your death
falls through the net
of my words

my words
try to hold you
fail yet again

I can only hold you
in these tears
this pain

your absence
hurting me
with its presence

LAST LONELY FLIGHT

Butterflies that flew in 1932
still held in that summer

by the exquisitely neat calligraphy
& cruel glinting pin.

I wipe the dust from the glass
& they gleam as if they still dream

of being alive.

I smash the glass
clutch them in my hand & climb

from attic to roof & slowly

drawing myself up to
my full height

release them back into time
smile as they flutter in the summer breeze

of then & now
their dead eyes taking it all in

clouds...trees...skies

their one last lonely flight
back into nothingness.

HWAET SEAL IC SINGAN? SING ME FRUMSCHAFT!

(What shall I sing...
. . .sing me creation!)

And she sang to him.
And she sang of him.

She sang of the love she had created for them.

She used birds for words & the rain that had fallen.
She used flowers & tears & interwove them.

She used sighs & hours & the loneliness within them.
She used moonlight & pain & what remained

...when she was far from him.

She sang of a love that had dreamed of being
...& hadn't yet awoken.

She sang of herself & called to him ....called to him.

And she sang of him.
And she sang to him.

She sang of the love ...that belonged to them.

She sealed it with tears & the fears of her heart
...breaking.

She sang him

Creation!